ᐸ

TRANSFORMATION MINDSET

10 Things Leaders should be Doing Today to turn Crisis into Opportunity

Laurence Smith

Contents

Foreword

The world needs leadership, now more than ever (during this pandemic).

We need to look up to someone (anyone, really) to give us the reassurance that everything will be OK. We need someone who seems to know what they are doing, even if they don't.

If you look at our current leaders around the world, they tended to have succeeded in their leadership because we, the people, needed them to. We needed our leaders to be successful, so we have given them the benefit of the doubt and have become less critical of them. Without them, mass panic could set in and we know it.

Bad leaders are being viewed as OK, OK leaders are viewed as good and good leaders as great. It seems that if you are currently the president or prime minister of a country, all you had to do is to not screw up. Apart from a few notable exceptions (yes, we all know who they are), country leaders have performed well enough to get us through the worst of the pandemic. Post pandemic however, the story might be different and only time will tell.

Does this correlate to business leaders? Are they experiencing these tailwinds and are their staff and shareholders being more sympathetic? From what I've seen, I think that most leaders are weathering the initial storm quite well, apart from the odd few who may have badly handled the furloughing of staff, either through mass firing over Zoom or forcing staff to leave rather then being made redundant to avoid bad press.

I know what you're thinking: why would I need to read a book about leadership if leaders are seen in a positive light and their followers are being supportive? Well the truth is, the game has changed and leaders are again being critically measured.

Now the green shoots are appearing, businesses are gearing up and quite frankly, the world as we know it has changed. We have seen massive acceleration of digitization, with the experts saying that two years' worth of digital transformation has occurred within just two months.

You may feel that the technology aspect of your organization has improved, but could you say the same for your company culture? I would say no, and if anything, it has regressed. Now is the time for you to accelerate all those other parts of your organization outside just technology.

The lessons contained in this book are simple, effective, and represent what the best-in-class organizations are already doing to gain agility and increase the productivity of a company's greatest asset, their staff.

In my mind, all a leader has to do, is to inspire their staff to do their career's best work. This, combined with an effective digital transformation, will turn any company into a leader in their industry and maybe even into the world's best!

Neal Cross
Co-founder & Chairman PictureWealth
Razer Fintech Advisory Board
Multi award winning Global Innovator
The 'World's Most Disruptive Chief Innovation Officer'
Social Entrepreneur

Saturday June 13th 2020

Advance Praise for
Transformation Mindset

"Laurence is one of the most forward thinking, transformation specialists in the world.

I've had the opportunity to closely work with Laurence for several years, and his deep knowledge and experience of how to strategically plan and drive real change within a company, is on par with the best McKinsey can offer.

As companies prepare for a very different world post the pandemic, this book's advice should be required reading for leaders everywhere."

Frank Meehan
Founder of Equilibrium.World, Partner SparkLabs Group.
Previously Boards of Spotify, Siri.

"Laurence Smith is one of Southeast Asia's best thought leaders on technology, HR and business organisations. For years he has challenged the status quo and taken audiences out of their comfort zones as a keynote speaker. Behind the scenes, I have benefited from his depth of experience and sound judgment.

Now we get finally get the book!

Laurence Smith's 10 Transformations are a "must know" list for businesses large and small."

Bob Aubrey
Founder and Strategic Advisor, the ASEAN Human
Development Organisation.

"Someone has been playing around with my wrist-watch (yes, I still have one).

I am positive that the mechanism is running faster now than it did last year, and I have a hunch that it will run faster again next year. Quite frankly, I just don't have the time that I used to have, and it's when I read excellent books like this one from Laurence Smith that it reminds me why. It would appear that it isn't my watch that's to blame after all....

In 10 simple yet powerful sections, Laurence provides a helpful overview of why things are changing so fast and how we experience it, along with an equal number of advisories on what we can do to keep pace. These are coping strategies for some, and clarion calls to personal re-invention for others. I can highly recommend it to anyone with the same faulty wrist-watch as me.

And if you need the wake-up call of this book, then you've probably already overslept. So get reading."

Reg Bull
GDHR Al-Futtaim Group, and 4x CHRO

"Laurence is one of the experts in the digital transformation field who not only understands the concept, but has also implemented it. So, I was delighted when he told me about this book project.

In this short Book, I have learned many practical tips I can apply (or recommend to my clients) immediately. My favorite one is LSE cycle – find out more in the book!

So, buy it and read it!

Then, implement what you find relevant for your circumstances. Transformation starts with the right mindset, and the results come from the actions you take. This Book will help you achieve that!"

Chutchapol Youngwiriyakul
Practice Leader, Kincentric

"We sit at a unique time where an organization's success can be made or broken overnight. Laurence's perspective on this topic comes from a stellar career in the Transformation and Change, Learning & Development and HR consulting arenas across Asian and Western multinationals."

Matt Chapman
Founder and Chairman of ChapmanCG & Chapman Ventures.

Acknowledgements & Thanks

As this is my first book, modest effort though it be, there are many influences that have led me here. I am sure I will miss a few, but here goes:

Firstly, Paul Howell who generously gave his time as Editor.

Orri Helgason who originally provoked me to think of this as a good idea…

Uma Rudd-Chia whose book '10 Things Brands can do to Survive a Crisis' directly inspired me.

Bob Aubrey who advised me on the challenges and lessons learned of writing and authoring – and always amazes me on how many books he authors!

The 200+ friends and ex-colleagues on LinkedIn and Facebook who shared their ideas and opinions on the front cover!

PixelStudio and HighDef, 2 great freelance talents on fiverr.com who designed the cover and formatted the book respectively.

Akash Karia of PublishingAccelerator.com for his advice on marketing the book and getting it into your hands.

My parents, especially my father David H Smith, who also spent a lifetime helping companies better learn, transform, innovate and better leverage technology – and inadvertently got me started on this path by giving me Toffler, Drucker and Handy to read as a teenager!

My various bosses, colleagues, and partners in my career to date. I've learned something from each of you, sometimes the hard way, but I would not be here without those challenges, highs and lows, failures and accomplishments.

Wow. When you actually stop to really think about all the people that have influenced your life and your career, that have challenged and inspired you, you realise that there really are far too many to recognise and name - but by golly, if they all buy a copy - this will definitely be a bestseller!

With thanks to you all.
Laurence Smith
Bali, June 12th 2020

ps. *And finally with thanks to my amazing kids, Jasmine and Hayden, as their school bills always inspire me to keep working harder than I ever expected!*

Prologue

We live in unprecedented times. We are all living through a crisis such that the world has never known before, and few, if any, of us were prepared for. The world beyond this pandemic will be very different, with fundamental changes in our work, businesses, societal engagements, and our very lives.

While we are all busy working to survive this crisis, care for loved ones, and keep our companies afloat, it is also a time of unprecedented opportunities – an opportunity to turn crisis into transformation, to develop smarter, more agile, more purpose-driven organisations, and more committed and engaged workforces than ever before.

This book is a provocation – and hopefully an inspiration – to get you thinking about some things you can do now that will increase the fitness and adaptability of your organisation, and increase the chances for your growth and success as we emerge into a very new and different world that will present a whole set of new challenges for leaders and HR.

By thinking about this now, and trying some of the ideas in this book, you will increase the resilience of your organisation and it's fitness to not just survive, but even thrive, thru and post this crisis.

1. Start with Purpose – and move away from *managing by presence*...

In the years to come, someone will analyse which companies survived this crisis best and emerged the strongest, and which ones floundered and sank.

I have a hypothesis that those companies with the strongest sense of "Purpose" embedded throughout their organisations, will be those that emerge the strongest. Organisations that still rely on traditional means of command and control will flounder. Those that can only "manage by presence" and have never built trust with their teams will struggle to cope with everyone suddenly working from home, and will revert to a panopticon of technologies to try to exert their control remotely to cover their own anxieties.

Here's the why and the how, by which you can strengthen the sense of Purpose in your organisation.

CEO Paul Polman performed a massively successful transformation at Unilever by taking the organisation back to its roots. He looked deep into why the organisation existed, what value it bought to the world, and its ability to positively effect people's lives all over the world.

Inspired by the scale and success of the transformation, I engaged the same partner, Nick Craig of the Core Leadership

Institute in Boston, to work with the CEO and Leadership team at DBS Bank. At the time, I was the Head of Learning and Talent Development, and charged with driving the rollout of the bank's new PRIDE Values, the 'P' standing for Purpose.

In a two-day period, Nick took the CEO and top 20 of the bank's Leadership Team deep into their own reasons for being at DBS, why they cared so deeply, and what motivated them to continue working so hard when they were each already so successful.

Amazingly, what emerged was that all 20 were there for the same reason. They all felt grateful for the opportunities they'd been given and the success they'd had. They all wanted to give back, and they all felt that DBS offered the best platform to do so. Each of them developed their own personal 'Life Purpose' statement, each unique, but all aligned with the same sense of good fortune, obligation, and opportunity.

On the second day Nick led them in an examination of: "Why work at DBS?" What value did DBS bring to it's customers, and what would happen if DBS ceased to exist? How long would it take customers to replace what DBS offered?

The group then turned these answers into a compelling Purpose Statement for DBS itself.

They talked about "weaving the bank into people's lives" and of "being the Google of banking" (remember, this was back in 2015).

Ultimately, they came up with the crazy, and clearly ridiculous, idea of *"Making Banking Joyful"*. Now for anyone who has ever experienced shock over unexpected bank fees, queued for hours in a branch, or waited for the call center to answer while listening to that awful music – or, even worse, got caught in the endless roundabout of automated phones systems – this idea was corporate insanity – people generally hate their banks, or at least do whatever possible to avoid having to deal with them.

And these guys were talking about '*making banking joyful*'? Were they crazy?

But what was funny is that when we shared this with people, and put together bank wide programmes to make it real, it resonated with people at a deeply personal level.

In conjunction with an existing obsession with Customer Journeys and the removal of 250 million hours of waste and customer wait time, we aimed to give employees back 1 million hours. Not a million hours of vacation time, but to remove 1,000,000 hours of bureaucracy; of make work tasks; of unnecessary paperwork.

Ref:

https://www.forbes.com/sites/jasonbloomberg/2016/12/23/how-dbs-bank-became-the-best-digital-bank-in-the-world-by-becoming-invisible/#17554a53061e

Realistically staff will not (be able to) care about making banking joyful for customers unless working at the bank is equally joyful.

"Making Banking Joyful" became an amazingly simple yet powerful decision-making framework. "Will doing this make banking more joyful for customers (or employees)?" If yes, let's do it, if not, let's re-think.

When people have such a powerful sense of Purpose, that acts as a simple decision-making mechanism: you have to worry less about how they will manage their time and work remotely, as they are both intrinsically motivated and self-guided.

Likewise, and most importantly for the current crisis situation we all find ourselves in, it became a "One True North" of alignment. Every staff member knew why the bank existed, what value it bought to customers and community, and what their role was in making that happen. They knew that there was a genuine and ongoing "Future of Work" initiative aimed at continuously making their working lives better, and that they were often invited to participate in such initiatives and be part of the solution.

Now, five year later, this has morphed into **"Live More, Bank Less"** and **"Making Banking Disappear"** and in recognition of its digital advancements, DBS became the world's first bank to hold three global best bank honours at the same time.

Ref:
https://www.youtube.com/watch?v=IiEMFdL6fKg&list=PLfOz-dEXVHj78JI1p4Zq69miPIRWAlog3A

In 2019, the business was named the World's Best Bank by *Euromoney,* following Global Bank of the Year from *The Banker,* and Best Bank in the World from *Global Finance,* both in 2018.

The takeaway here is that when there is true and em-bedded Purpose, and when the values, culture, leadership behaviours, and all the HR systems and processes are aligned to support it, people are far more engaged, self-motivated, internally-driven and likely to work hard to achieve their goals – whether in the office and supervised, or working from home while also managing kids, spouses, and pets.

The reality is that the old command and control models stopped working years ago, but we never knew a better way. Well – in the brave new world post crisis, those organisations that have the strongest real sense of Purpose, and supporting culture and systems, will out-perform those that relied on command and control.

So the question is, does your organisation have a strong enough and compelling enough sense of Purpose, truly em-bedded and lived, that your employees don't just know what to do in this crisis, but know how to do it, and are motivated enough to care and follow through? If not, you might want to consider working on it now. There is no better time to focus on and show you are serious about Purpose than right now.

Late News Flash — just made it into print!

And for the best news, in a conversation with Nick just the other day, I was most surprised to learn that this programme, which I have personally experienced, face to face, as the most intense personal development programme I had ever done, can also be done virtually.

Indeed Nick and his team are currently doing a whole series of sessions virtually for one of the world's most innovative manufacturers, and it's been so successful that they are actually increasing the number of programmes they are doing during the crisis to be ready to really to explode off the starting blocks as we move beyond this 'Great Transformation.'

Recommended Reading:

Leading from Purpose: Clarity and the Confidence to Act When It Matters Most

Ref: <u>Forbes: Can DBS Make Banking Joyful?</u>

https://www.forbes.com/sites/jonathansalembaskin/2015/12/21/can-dbs-make-banking-joyful/#4fc6b0aa9888

Recommended Resource: Core Leadership Institute

2. Are your values ready for today's world?

As a follow-on to the absolute importance of Purpose outlined above, it is critical that our overall corporate values are aligned, lived, and bought to life by every policy, process, and behavior throughout the organisation.

In this time of crisis, you may be re-evaluating your corporate values, realising that people are not really living them – or that they don't suit today's reality – and are therefore evolving them to align with this new world. If you're changing how you work, manage and lead, then you need to evolve your organisation's values, and this definitely needs to be a collaborative virtual process involving as many employees as possible, so it is something they really own – and not just 'buy into.'

Why do organisations even need values? Simplistically speaking, organisations have values to guide managers and employees on how to best behave in line with the company's vision and purpose.

If we break that down further, keeping it simple, there's really two reasons values are helpful. They provide:

- Nudges and reminders on how to behave when nobody is looking; and

- Guidance on how to decide and act in situations of novelty and ambiguity

Well guess what? Today, nobody is looking – as everyone is working remotely. And we are without doubt living through the greatest period of doubt, fear, uncertainty, and ambiguity most of us have ever dealt with. So I would argue that getting our values "right" and lived by everyone, has never been more important.

But how to do that when nobody is at the office?

There's a fairly quick and effective way to either define new values, evolve existing values, or get more specific about how to live values and bring them to life in this new world of remote work and management by Purpose.

I think it was back in 2003 when IBM ran their first global online "Values Jam" to totally transform the values of IBM and help them succeed in a very different world of technology and business in the 21st Century. They involved over 100,000 people globally in a multi-day online discussion forum (or "Jam"), where they worked to identify the new values and define what it meant to bring them to life, and live them in the world of everyday work.

A decade or so later, I proposed, designed and ran a similar process at DBS Bank in Asia, as we evolved and rolled out a new set of values with the acronym "PRIDE". In the first instance, and almost as an experiment (or proof of concept), we tried this over three days with the top 200+ Managing Directors, and were pleasantly surprised with the degree of participation from the most senior people in the company.

This helped us refine what we meant by each of the PRIDE Values, and gave us a perspective from all the countries across Asia and every department of the bank.

In a follow-up session a few months later, we engaged all 22,000 staff across 15 countries in a week long virtual Values Jam to go deeper. We leveraged an online platform with channels and content for each of the Values, and focused on a different one each day, whilst allowing people to browse all the values and ideas and contribute wherever something caught their eye.

By the end of the week we'd had contributions from thousands of employees, and amazing ideas from every country, department and team. The outcome was better-defined values with shared agreement on what it meant to bring them to life, and lots of examples of where it was already happening. Throughout the bank, people felt that these values really resonated with them and reflected the reality of life at work as they had a hand in defining and shaping them.

Looking at your organisation today, are your existing values fit for purpose in a world of remote working, virtual meetings, and where managers are having to work with and mange people in totally different ways?

If not, you can do a relatively quick and simple version of the Values Jam described above to strengthen people's alignment and engagement.

Values Jam NOW

There are lots of ways to design this, but here's just one idea.

Take some staff who are currently under-utilised and empower them to lead an online company-wide Values Jam.

Give them the appropriate sponsorship and some resources, as well as a short timeframe to come back to you with three or four suggestions. Have them leverage design thinking principles, and ideally design and run some quick experiments to get reactions from employees on which ideas they like best.

In other words, use this process as an opportunity to get people thinking like a startup, generating initial ideas, building some quick prototypes and running some experiments to get validation and data.

Once you get some feedback from different employee

groups, have the team present the two best ideas to a panel of leaders and employees to decide which to roll out. Now you're essentially running a (very simplistic) lean startup process, and have gotten as many people involved as possible.

Once you have a preferred mode for the Values Jam, enrol everyone who participated in the initial experiments and design as champions to help roll it out. It is critical that if you are trying to develop values that will enable a more inclusive, innovative, purpose driven, self-motivated, high employee experience workplace, then the process itself must both mirror and model the types of outcomes you're looking for.

You can run this as an iterative process: agreeing first upon the key values that matter to people; then later refining them to more clarity in terms of definitions.

If you have the time and resources, the definitions can be defined at the individual, team and organisational levels. For example at DBS Bank we defined 'Decisiveness' (the D in PRIDE), in terms of how people would think of that at a personal level, as a member of a team, and on behalf of the whole organisation. This helped people think beyond them-selves and also consider what is better or best for those larger bodies, versus perhaps shying away from responsibility or opportunity by arguing that it's beyond their level or mandate.

It is important that the values, behaviours and responses are not defined by seniority, but rather encourage everyone to think holistically.

Another key point is to define the behaviours expected in terms that maximise the probability that people will ac-cept and internalise them, and act accordingly. So try not to describe the behaviours in "do this" and "don't do that" terms – which can be quite authoritarian and implies that what they have been doing in the past was wrong and that they should stop it. This is guaranteed to invoke an invol-untary threat response as you essentially criticise people's previous behaviour.

Instead, describe the new behaviours in terms of "do more of this" and "do less of that", so that people understand that times have changed and that their behaviour needs to change with it. Linguistically and neurologically it's much less threatening; even encouraging.

They don't have to be perfect immediately, but as they go along, try to do more of the new behaviours, and let go of the older, less functional behaviours. (With thanks to David Rock one of the leading thinkers on applying neuroscience to organisations, and Founder of the NeuroLeadership Institute, who worked with us on this).

Another step can be enrolling as many people as possible to add examples of where such behaviours are already common in the organisation. This can either be an activity in the Values Jam, or a follow up, or even as an ongoing activity.

Ideally while operating under crisis conditions, you are continuing to collect, communicate and share great examples of where people are going above and beyond in customer service and business growth. Please also do so for examples that bring the values to life and demonstrate the behaviours you want everyone to adopt.

In summary, some empowered, self-directed teams with appropriate executive sponsorship can have a big impact on employee morale, engagement, and experience by helping evolve the values to better suit the new organisation you are becoming and the behaviours you all need to succeed.

3. Transparency breeds trust

Many business leaders and owners are currently struggling with laying people off, or telling them they can't pay them. This is the worst possible time for anyone to lose their job and income, and for many the meaning they get from work is also critical to their self image, mental health, and wellbeing.

If you are a leader in this position, be open and transparent about the challenges you face. Your employees are smart people, they know these times are hard for every business. If you give them the chance, they will help you come up with solutions.

Traditional command and control style leaders simply see people as costs, and do their best to control these costs at all times. In these difficult times, they will simply cut people as the quickest way to survival. But I would argue that it is precisely these types of organisations – and these types of leaders – that will not survive this crisis, or if by some miracle they do, will be unable to attract the best talent and thereby perform the most poorly in tomorrow's new world of work.

A *Harvard Business Review* assessment of corporate performance during the past three recessions found that, of the 4,700 firms studied, those that cut costs fastest and deepest had the lowest probability of outperforming competitors after the economy recovered. (Ranjay Gulati, Nitin Nohria, and Franz Wohlgezogen, "Roaring out of recession," *Harvard Business Review*, March 2010).

Trust your employees, especially if you have built a Purpose-driven organisation and have developed a culture of trust: it will pay back dividends in these times. Ask your staff for what to do, how to cut costs, how to improve the businesses, how to reach out to customers, and how to re-negotiate or build stronger partnerships with suppliers.

In some organisations I know, staff have taken voluntary pay cuts to avoid cutting fellow employees. In one great example, all staff agreed to take cuts, but due to everyone's differing circumstances, each took the cut they could afford by submitting it confidentially to HR in writing. Overall, it averaged a 20% pay cut across the board: the company is still going strong, and nobody lost their job.

There are hundreds of ideas floating around in the heads of your employees as to how, if only someone would listen or give them a chance, they could save a dollar here, improve a product there, delight a customer, or come up with some new innovation.

Now is not the time to batten the hatches and hunker down, but rather the time to open up. Ask employees for their greatest contribution. Ask leaders to lead by example and make themselves vulnerable by admitting that nobody has all the answers, but know that the wisdom of the crowd, of employees and other stakeholders, when bought together, can result in amazing ideas, innovations and cost savings.

Leverage online innovation and crowdsourcing platforms to develop, filter and assess ideas from across the organisation. Make it open and involve employees, in every step of the process. Let them help vote or decide what gets implemented; let them develop the metrics and dashboards that track the results; share the impact and cost savings.

Ask for their hearts and minds as well as their hands, and people will step forward and surprise and delight you. And that will help your organisation can emerge from this crisis stronger than ever and better positioned to innovate and compete.

In one of their recent articles, Deloitte explain it quite nicely:

"In a time of crisis, trust is paramount. This simple formula emphasises the key elements of trust for individuals and for organizations:

Trust = Transparency + Relationship + Experience

Trust starts with transparency: telling what you know and admitting what you don't. Trust is also a function of relationships: some level of "knowing" each other among you and your employees, your customers, and your ecosystem. And lastly, it also depends on experience: Do you reliably do what you say? In times of growing uncertainty, trust is increasingly built by demonstrating an ability to address unanticipated situations and a steady commitment to address the needs of all stakeholders in the best way possible."

Ref:

https://www2.deloitte.com/us/en/insights/economy/covid-19/heart-of-resilient-leadership-responding-to-covid-19.html

Reflection

So if you think about the first three chapters, they all lead towards what Deloitte is talking about here. Purpose-driven organisations, with aligned values lived consistently through the organisation, and which communicate transparently with employees, will be best placed to live through this crisis and be part of the transformation journey in the post-Covid world.

4. Developing a Gig Mindset* – Do you really have to own them all?

Just as the world is increasingly moving to rent services on demand: Uber; Airbnb, UpWork, 99Designs and the like; do you really need all your employees to be "employees"?

Given the immense cost pressures everyone is under these days, and if you're faced with potentially laying people off (as discussed above), consider one more option.

Offer some of your existing employees the opportunity to start their own business providing the same services back to you, but without the fixed costs and overheads they would cost you as an employee. Of course, you'd want to guarantee them a certain amount of work for a reasonable time period to give them the courage to take this step.

This could allow people that had always wanted to, but never had the courage or resources, to finally become an entrepreneur and start their own business. Not only does it reduce your fixed costs and headcount, but as these people are now also serving other clients, the chances are they are being exposed to more new ideas, learning faster, and becoming ever more skilled at the services they also do for you. So, done right, everyone could win.

Think of these people as part of your eco-system of "community and crowd." They are emotionally aligned to you, flexible to provide the services you require, and constantly up-skilling themselves at their own expense.

Taking advantage of the gig economy does not mean you always have to work with strangers. What part of your business is open to leveraging – or providing services and resources, to the larger business eco-system? For some organisations, there could be whole new revenue opportunities here.

Sharing your employees

Interestingly, in China where they are ahead of the curve in responding to Coronavirus and coming out the other side earlier, some companies are taking really innovative approaches to employees and staffing. In *HBR* for example:

"Rapid, coordinated responses require top-down leadership. But adapting to unpredictable change, with distinct dynamics in different communities, also requires decentralised initiative-taking. Some Chinese companies effectively balanced the two approaches, setting a top-down framework within which employees innovated.

For example, Huazhu, which operates 6,000 hotels in 400 cities across China, set up a crisis task force that met daily to review procedures and issued top-down guidance for the whole chain. In addition, it leveraged its internal information platform, an app called Huatong, to make sure employees and franchisees were armed with timely information. This allowed franchisees to adapt central guidance to their own local situations, in terms of disease conditions and local public health measures."

Ref:
https://hbr.org/2020/03/how-chinese-companies-have-responded-to-coronavirus

Lending, leasing and redeploying staff

MIT Sloan quotes other examples from China and Europe,

where companies have been "leasing" staff to each other to balance supply and demand under various different lockdown situations.

"When Alibaba's supermarket chain Hema found itself in urgent need of labour to meet demand, it turned to an innovative "employee sharing plan" to "borrow" more than 3,000 employees made temporarily redundant from jobs in restaurants, hotels, and movie theater chains.

"In Germany, McDonald's staff have been given permission to work at Aldi stores while the fast-food chain's restaurants are shut. Aldi has been overwhelmed by demand as grocery shopping has significantly increased during the pandemic. The employee-leasing agreement is for a limited period only, and all those who apply can simply return to McDonald's once their restaurants reopen."

Ref:

https://sloanreview.mit.edu/article/three-proactive-response-strategies-to-covid-19-business-challenges/

In addition, the *South China Morning Post* reports that:

> *"What appeared to be a well-meaning gesture to share labour costs in times of great financial distress has far-reaching implications in terms of management and corporate social responsibility.*
>
> *In extending a helping hand, Hema served as an online platform for allocating excess economic resources, becoming a middleman directing idle resources to where there was critical need.*
>
> *Hema's example led to a raft of similar moves by companies such as Shunliban, JD 7Fresh, Suning and Lenovo. Suning Logistics reportedly posted job openings for courier, warehouse sorter and part-time call centre staff in anticipation of a spike in "shared employment".*
>
> *These corporations are using the internet as a testing ground for novel notions and practices in human resource management."*

Ref:

https://www.scmp.com/comment/opinion/article/3077417/chi-nas-coronavirus-hit-companies-internet-can-be-much-more-just

What I love about all these examples from China is that they demonstrate the flexibility of mindset and culture of experimentation that we have traditionally associated with Silicon Valley, and I think these examples show the way forward for us all.

Seek community support; engage customers and stakeholders

Do not limit this openness and collective wisdom only to your employees. You can extend the same thinking beyond the organisation to your customers, partners, suppliers, and community.

Use this as an opportunity to have radically open conversations where you previously negotiated hard. Everyone is suffering, even those companies like Amazon or food delivery firms who cannot meet demand. Have open conversations, and develop some real win–win scenarios and partnerships that can develop into trusted relationships.

Use this opportunity to get closer than ever (virtually of course), to customers, and really understand why they use your products.

Ask, why do they work with you and not your competitors? What's the real JTBD (Jobs to be Done) that your product or service fulfils in their lives – and how can you make it even better or more useful to them? How can you digitise these products and services? How can you add value by adding data? What data do you have about your customers needs, usage metrics, impact and measurement that they don't have or that you don't normally share. What extra value could you deliver to them by increasing the use of data and dashboards into your operating relationship?

Ref:

*https://www.amazon.com/Gig-Mindset-Reclaim-Reinvent-Disruption-ebook/dp/B082QN2DJ6/ref=sr_1_1?crid=3UZBM6VKGX-K3A&dchild=1&keywords=gig+mindset&qid=1590305012&s=digital-text&sprefix=gig+%2Caps%2C421&sr=1-1

5. Learn, share and experiment

Your business is being disrupted by a Black Swan event few of us predicted – and certainly none of us were ready for. Nobody really knows what is going to happen next.

Is this a Great Transformation as some have argued; will there be a "new normal" or will the post-Covid world be something no-one has yet predicted. Facebook, Google, Twitter and others, have already announced that employees can work from home until the end of 2020. The Future of Work is finally here, but not in the way any of us predicted.

So how do we take advantage of this uncertainty? How do we turn this period of ambiguity into an opportunity to be better prepared for whatever's next?

It's highly probable that some of your employees are currently under-utilised. Here's a great way to engage them, develop them, and help the whole organisation be better prepared to compete in the post-Covid world.

In your organisation you can implement what I call **LSE Cycles,** standing for *"Learn, Share, and Experiment"*.

This is an accelerated methodology by which an organisation can quickly get up to speed on the potential impact and opportunity offered by emerging technologies, as well as increase the knowledge and awareness of the organisation.

Done right, you are likely to also get some new product and solution innovations occurring as a result.

Every phase has a different objective, each of which feeds into the next phase. I call them "cycles" because the highest impact occurs when you run multiple loops through them, leading to incremental, and sometimes exponential, impact and learning.

The Learning Phase

Start by forming virtual teams of eight to 16 people from across the business. They should be as diverse as possible in every way. There are no pre-requisites to joining but, at this stage at least, try to avoid people that are known deniers of digital or resisters of change.

In face-to-face hackathons (which are somewhat similar), teams of eight seem to be ideal, but given that this is virtual, larger teams of 12 to 16 are preferred. These will allow breakout groups to focus on different areas, all coordinated around different time zones and existing work commitments.

In this first phase, teams are tasked to immerse themselves in the target technology. They should learn as much as they can, and start to think about the potential implications for society, their industry, and their customers.

You can create your own list of technologies that you believe are most relevant, but let me offer some suggestions:

- Artificial intelligence, Machine Learning and Big Data
- Augmented and Virtual Reality
- 3D Printing
- Industrial Robots
- Drones
- 5G
- Sensors and the Internet of Things
- Solar energy
- Autonomous vehicles

- Blockchain
- Biotech

Whichever you choose as most relevant to your industry, throw in at least one wildcard as well, something that is not obviously relevant. Sometimes the best insights come from unexpected directions.

Give the team 72 hours to one week, no longer, to research the technology and understand where it is going, and the potential implications for your business. A very powerful framework I like to use is the **6Ds Framework** from Peter Diamandis, of Singularity University.

The **6Ds** are **Digitized, Deceptive, Disruptive, Dematerialize, Demonetize** and **Democratize**.

The logic is that as technologies become *Digitized*, they enter a period of *Deceptive* growth, where they may well be doubling in efficiency every 12 to 18 months (like Moore's Law), but they are starting from such a low base that there is no apparent impact for quite a while and people often dismiss their potential for impact.

Indeed, as Bill Gates said:

"We always overestimate the change that will occur in the next two years and underestimate the change that will occur in the next ten."

Then these technologies reach a point in the curve where they are suddenly *Disruptive* to established players, and this typically take companies by surprise. The examples are many, Kodak ignoring the very digital camera they invented; Blockbuster refusing to buy NetFlix for $50m – (NetFlix is now worth nearly US$200b and Blockbuster is long since bankrupt); Nokia, Blackberry, and Steve Ballmer of Microsoft denigrating the first iPhone as a "toy". You probably have your own favourite example.

Before the teams present their findings, you want them to come up with a hypothesis on at least one way the technology could disrupt a key part of your business, launch a new product, or enter a totally new market. In phase three, experimentation, they will set about testing that hypothesis.

The Sharing Phase

To misquote Ernest Hemingway, "*Disruption happens slowly, then suddenly*". This LSE initiative is how you avoid your company being blindsided by technology moving from its *Deceptive* to *Disruptive* phase.

Your teams should each come up with a briefing on their selected technology, which includes some of the potential implications for you and your customers. Challenge them to present their findings back to the organisation in imaginative ways, which ideally need to be interactive as there are three objectives here.

Firstly, you want the teams to prove what they've learned by "teaching it back" through the sharing sessions. If made interesting, fun, and interactive (which is the second objective), then a larger part of the organisation will learn as well – a powerful secondary benefit and multiplier of potential impact.

Thirdly, these sessions are an opportunity to test the ideas, gain new input from more people, and recruit additional members and even sponsors for the next phase of experiments.

The Experimenting Phase

This is the most fun and may require some small amount of resources and budget. As the teams share their findings, you may well have attracted the attention of business leaders who can envisage the potential of these technologies, and will step forward with business challenges to solve and/or the resources to sponsor the next phase.

Each team should now come up with one or more experiments that will prove their initial hypothesis about how a particular technology, or technologies, could disrupt the business or create new opportunities.

In these experiments you are looking for data; validated learnings that these ideas would appeal to customers. You need to get enough insights to know whether you should pivot or persevere (pursue this product/idea, or morph it into something different based on the feedback).

When we did this with face-to-face hacakthons of combined teams of senior bankers and startups at DBS bank, there was an amazing variety of experiments run. We had teams overnight build landing pages to exhibit their potential solutions and buy Google Ad words or Facebook advertising to drive traffic from potential customers. They then analysed whether people clicked on "learn more", "register here", and "buy now" options, and developed data-based insights as to how people interacted, and the percentage of potential customers within the sample.

A number of famous companies have actually started this way: by building a landing page and simply seeing whether they got enough hits and signups to make it worth building the product as described. This is a high speed, super-cheap way to test and validate some assumption about how a particular technology could impact your business, and develop some innovative new products and solutions that could meet new customer needs.

In the Lean Startup world they literally call this "the Landing Page" and it's a very simple form of a Minimal Viable Product (MVP) test. An MVP is the simplest prototype, that you can build super quickly and cheaply, and can test your most basic assumptions.

Here's a good definition of the Landing Page MVP from Openclassrooms.com

"A landing page is a single page that:

- *Describes your product or service*

- *Illustrates some advantages of using your product or service (your "unique value proposition")*
- *Contains a button that lets interested visitors click to read more, join a mailing list, buy now, or some other action*

The big advantages of using landing pages are:

- *Landing pages contain a description of why your service is compelling. You can see if your unique value proposition resonates with customers very early in the process.*
- *By using multiple landing pages, you can see which messaging resonates better with customers.*
- *You can capture the email addresses of interested people, which will allow you to follow up and do interviews with them later.*
- *Landing pages can be created in a few hours. If you can spend roughly $100 in Google Ads to generate some visitors, then you can get data the same day. That is completing the whole lean cycle in just one day!"*

Ref:
https://openclassrooms.com/en/courses/4544561-learn-about-lean-startup/4703206-discover-the-4-types-of-minimum-viable-product

There are many more types of experiments and MVPs that can get data to prove or disprove their hypothesis, but the most important thing is that they are learning by doing. They are sharing and spreading what they are learning, are addressing some real business challenges and opportunities at the same time, giving you a window into the future of how exponential technologies could affect your business.

In effect, this is an accelerated version of Google's famous "20% Time" to innovate, which is credited with launching so many new products. But you can run it now, and do it virtually, while people are not fully engaged at their desks.

Some of your staff will get super excited about LSE cycles and want to participate in multiple projects, and for others, it will be a useful learning experience and they will move on. Keep track of those that are good at this. They are likely to be more innovative and creative, and generate more ideas in the future. They could well be worth considering for any Fast-Track or Top Talent programmes you have.

The other 3Ds

Those of you paying attention will note that I only talked about the first 3Ds of the Peter Diamandis model. They are sufficient on their own to take teams a long way in their thinking. The next 3Ds are much more dramatic in their impact, and much more transformational in terms of where your organisation could go in the future.

I will explain them briefly here, but I would encourage you to read more, or contact me if you want to learn more, or work with them further.

The next 3Ds are **Dematerialise, Demonetise** and **Democratise**.

Dematerialise represents the dramatic impact when products go from physical to digital and can be reproduced, distributed and shared, at zero marginal cost. Obvious examples are books, music and movies, but also your smartphone. All the apps and services there used to be physical cameras, maps, books, records, and libraries. In fact, there's literally what was once hundreds of thousands of dollars of value, included free in your smartphone.

Demonetise is about what has happened to those apps on your smartphone, and the fact that they are all now available for free. Likewise, Uber, AirBnB and Skype are demonetizing the taxi, hotel and long distance industries respectively.

The last D is *Democratise*, and this one is astounding, as suddenly billions more people around the world have access to all the world's knowledge, computing on demand via Amazon Cloud and even AI as a Service. There's suddenly an extra couple of billion people with access to knowledge that was traditionally hoarded and controlled by governments and the largest of corporations.

Indeed, as Google's Project Loon and various near earth satellite projects bring internet access to everyone, a fascinating LSE cycle to run is to consider how your company might leverage these new technologies to serve the three billion new customers coming online in the next few years....

RedCells

One final idea. If you really want to ensure that your company is the most agile, adaptable, and fittest in your industry and ready to survive, create a Red Cell.

The "Red Cell" is originally a military concept of a small, secret team, given the mandate to break all the rules and do their best to – literally – blow up their home base. In this case, it is the parent organisation, department or business that is the target. It is the epitome of **Clayton Christensen's** spirit of *'disrupt or be disrupted.'*

IMD describes Red Cell teams as:

> *"The Red Cell is an idea borrowed from the military world and adapted for use in the business environment. It provides a competitive advantage due to two primary deliverables. Firstly, it provides a thorough and objective view of the environment from the standpoint of an outsider.*
>
> *This perspective may primarily be that of a competitor but could just as well be that of a customer, supplier, or regulator. Secondly, it confronts plans and strategies from this external perspective.*
>
> *In so doing it ensures that an organization does not develop a 'yes Sir' bureaucracy, but rather an environment of critical thinking and rigorous planning."*

Ref:
https://www.managementexchange.com/hack/red-cell

The logic behind this is that a Red Cell (like a red blood cell) is inside the organisation, and can best identify and expose all its weaknesses. This can also lessen the auto-rejection from the organisation immune system, but be aware that you need to be a confident leader to take this on.

A successful Red Cell will show how to cannibalise your most profitable products before your competitors can, and highlight gaps in strategy, market positioning, and leadership. For a leader with strong self-confidence and faith in their organisation, a Red Cell can also be a massive accelerator of organisational fitness.

Note that a Red Cell team can be even more powerful if the team goes beyond written reports and also deploys an LSE cycle as described above. It can then actually build prototypes or run some experiments to demonstrate their ideas. It is very hard to argue with real data from experiments versus the relative strengths of someone else's opinion.

Traditionally, feedback from Red Cell teams has often been strongly resisted by executives whose ideas, departments or businesses were the target and who could potentially lose face. By instead running this with experiments, and gathering data via validated learnings, this can result in a much "softer" but equally impactful shared learning experience, where the Red Cell team and the target business all learn and improve.

In fact, done right, the target executives can become the biggest fans of the Red Cell's insights. They need to grasp its lessons and insights quickly, and move to experiment further and deploy these solutions and ideas faster than their competitors.

6. Transform Faster – Get Digital Now

One thing that is certain today, is that moving forward there will be less resistance to all things virtual and digital. While in the short term people will be desperate to reconnect physically, to hold meetings and gatherings, and to rebuild physical communities, we will not forget what we have been exposed to digitally.

In one way this crisis has been a massive accelerator of "the Future of Work" and of 'Digital Transformation' in general. Indeed, Satya Nadella, CEO of Microsoft has just shared that the company has achieved more in terms of Digital Transformation in the last two months, than they had expected to achieve in the next 2 years.

Deniers, resisters and luddites of all things digital have had no choice but to use food delivery apps, online entertainment, video conferencing and other remote working tools. There will be no reversion to "how things were" or the "good old days". Managing by presence will never be as strong as before – and at the same time, more people will have been replaced by machines faster than expected, and will need support and re-skilling.

My suggestion? Move forward even faster. Explode out of the starting blocks when the new race starts. "Get Digital" even faster. Work harder to develop the "Digital Mindset" and capabilities of your leaders, talents and workforce even faster than the competition. Use this time now to increase their Digital Quotient and ability to learn, adapt and compete in this new world.

Try some experiments around prototyping, design thinking, mobile micro-learning, virtual hackathons, design-athons or make-athons. Bring people together in virtual teams and communities to try "digital by digital".

You could start by running an online suggestions box (or use an innovation crowdsourcing platform) to get ideas from all across the organisation on how to "Get Digital" faster. If you have a Talent Programme or Management Associates, give them the challenge to come up with ideas, experiments and prototypes.

Here's some things that work:

Back at DBS Bank we set the Management Associates (new Grads, fresh from University who were accepted into a fast track Management Development Programme), the task of helping the Leadership team "Get Digital' faster.

The MAs came up with some really simple ideas that worked well. One was to have each of them choose an app that they found useful in everyday life and do a quick, three-minute demo at the intersection of each session at the Management Offsite for the top 150 leaders. This was so simple, and worked so well, that many leaders, cascaded the practice back into their own countries or departments.

Reverse Mentoring

More formal reverse mentoring programmes also worked well, where you had junior talents coaching really senior people on digital, and picking up exposure and leadership wisdom in return. Again, if you have a fun and gamified micro-learning platform with relevant digital content, there is nobody more competitive than senior leaders, so leaderboard updates tracking who's got the most points really accelerates adoption, and people end up having huge fun getting digital.

Competitions, Campaigns & Challenges

Run a "Get Digital" campaign across multiple locations using a fun micro-learning platform (or your own LMS if it suits) with relevant, engaging content. Make it competitive, run it as a campaign – I use the term *"Campaignification"* for this process: that is, the gamification of the engagement campaign – so that employees actually find it both relevant and fun!

Leverage the leaderboard to have locations, teams or functions compete against each other and leverage people's natural competitiveness to have fun, learn, and connect over distance and feel human again!

One company I worked with did an Asia wide competition on Digital Mindset with their top 200 leaders across Singapore, Shanghai and Sydney. This was a week-long "Get Digital" campaign with all manner of virtual and live events, startup demos, entrepreneur briefings and fireside chats, as well as the week-long challenge driven by the leader board. Given the cultural diversity of the leaders involved, and the campaignification of the engagement process, it became tremendously competitive and the content library had to be added to twice in a week, as participation blew past all expectations.

I have seen companies use prizes as simple as Starbucks vouchers or as attention grabbing as new iPhones. I even remember one company that gave a day of leave for anyone who scored 10,000 points (obviously you will need to re-think what prizes make sense in today's world!) But the real prize is the sense of accomplishment people get from learning more – as well as beating their friends on the leaderboard!

Another company I worked with, a major global payments

company, ran a four-week "Get Digital" campaign across their top 400 leaders in Asia-Pacific. They structured it as "four weeks, four leaders, four themes". Each Monday, a senior leader would send an email to all 400 announcing the theme of the week, for example, "The Future of Payments" or "Company X in a FinTech World", plus a link to their interview on a mobile micro-learning platform★. This talked about that leader's vision of the future, the challenges, and the opportunities. It also included links to their favourite articles or inspiring videos. As well as some simple quizzes to test people's attention and help them internalise the knowledge.

The rest of the playlist for that week would be interviews with thought leaders, overviews of key tech trends, and deeper dives into transformational technologies. In addition there was, industry specific content, in this case profiles of emerging disrupters in the FinTech space.

Two things the leaders particularly loved were the polls – where they could do some quick surveys of the audience and where they thought the company was on its journey and how well they were doing – and the leaderboard, which driven by the learning, the polls and quizzes, drove extremely high levels of competitiveness across all participants.

Have different teams take it in turns to design some "Get Digital' challenges or tasks that each team has to compete. An online data scavenger hunt for example. You would be amazed by just how much information is out there about your own company, and the key competitors that you never knew existed. Have teams compete to find the dashboards and tools, and present to each other with judges and prizes, or just recognition on the table.

Challenge your Learning and Development team to col-laborate with the Innovation team to come up with some imaginative, and fun, initiatives to help people learn to love digital and remove the fear that has disabled so many up to now.

As you increase the digital literacy of your organisation,

things will start to spread of their own accord. Innovations will occur unexpectedly, and will spread from a mindset/ digital literacy thing to people fundamentally thinking about how to solve customers problems in new and unique ways leveraging digital and data.

Here's a great example of such innovation from China, which is ahead the rest of the world in facing these challenges and turning them into opportunities :

> *"When Chinese cosmetics company Lin Qingxuan was forced to close 40% of its stores, including all of its locations in Wuhan, sales plummeted by 90%. However, the company redeployed its beauty advisers as online influencers, leveraging digital tools such as WeChat to engage customers virtually and drive online sales. On Valentine's Day, Lin Qingxuan launched a large-scale, livestream shopping event featuring more than 100 beauty advisers; one adviser's sales in just two hours equaled that of four retail stores. The company's February sales <u>climbed 120%</u> over last year's."*

And one of my personal favourites, *"Meanwhile, vine-yards from Burgundy to Napa Valley are offering online wine-tasting lessons in combination with wine purchases and have seen sales explode. Similarly, London's Bimber Distillery, a whiskey maker, has canceled its distillery tours, instead delivering tasting kits to customers and running events online."*

Ref:

https://sloanreview.mit.edu/article/three-proactive-response-strategies-to-covid-19-business-challenges/

Recommended Reading:

Digital Mindset: 6 things that work

Recommended Resources:

SmartUp.io the mobile micro learning platform for 'Get Digital' challenges★ ★(Disclosure, I sit on the Advisory Board of SmartUp).

Orri Helgason: Worked with us as DBS to design & roll-out the hackathons across Asia, & is the best designer and facilitator of 'get digital' programmes I've worked with.

7. Digital Advisory Boards go Virtual

I've been fortunate to be involved with a few different Digital Advisory Board models over the last few years and if you don't have one, what follows are some ideas on how to quickly – and affordably – leverage some outside expertise to accelerate your transformation.

First of all though, what are Digital Advisory Boards (DABs) and why do they matter? DABs obviously come in all shapes and sizes, and just like many corporate innovation centers, can often fail miserably.

DABs are typically a combination of internal and external members meeting a few times a years to share, learn and problem-solve on different areas of the business where digital can have a significant impact.

They are often started by the marketing team, and sometimes keep their mandate rather narrowly defined as if "Digital Transformation" only applied to digital marketing.

Those that I've seen be most successful are generally those that have a broader organisational transformation mandate, while diving deep into specific areas or themes as needed. They then also benefit from broader, and more senior organisational sponsorship and consequently have a larger impact on the business as a whole.

The benefits of DABs are several-fold. They help you:

- Identify and understand emerging technologies, and how they might impact your customers, competitors and your own business.
- Understand how these technology trends can impact society as a whole, and the longer term societal implications.
- Leverage external and multi-industry expertise giving you both an outside-in perspective, as well as insights from both complementary/adjacent industries, and dramatically different industries, potentially leading to provocative new ideas and opportunities.
- Gain a better understanding of the ecosystem in which you and your partners operate, leading to new collaboration opportunities
- Develop greater customer intimacy as your different partners and advisory board members interact with your target audience from very different perspectives, enabling you to put yourself "in your customer's shoes" from multiple points of view.
- Reduce resistance to change and "digital denial" as you invite and involve different leaders and internal stakeholders to participate and learn.
- Institute more effective real-time problem solving, innovation and product development.
- Develop a faster cascading of digital literacy and mindset as more people participate and more problems are solved.
- Accelerated adoption of Digital Mindset organisation-wide

Selection of DAB members

Selection of DAB members initially requires a high level of internal sponsorship, typically a CEO or COO, though, as mentioned, it may well start with the CMO, before, ideally, broadening in sponsorship and mandate. It is critical that the body focuses on issues of strategic growth and transformative importance to the business. Note that this will evolve over time as the DAB launches, grows and eventually gains a track record of successes and impact: starting small and with an experimental mindset is totally fine here.

For internal members, there is a small core team of permanent members, one or more of whom will design and run the DAB. They will solicit input from the sponsor and key stakeholder on priority topics for the agenda, and source relevant external participants, again both core members and occasional invitees, as required.

For external members, you typically look for a combination of recognised external thought leadership who can bring both leading edge technology insights and implications, together with industry practitioners who have specific expertise and experience from adjacent and complementary industries. Adding an occasional "wild card" member can also be useful to shake up people's ideas and perspectives. This can be an entrepreneur or thought leader from totally different industries. I remember one multinational, who even included a 'corporate poet' for a very different take on things.

Prior operating models

Here's a very successful DAB operating model that I enjoyed a lot, as an example. Run over an evening and a full day, this would bring together people to solve specific market growth challenges, innovate, and quickly prototype new product ideas.

The first evening, members new and old, would all gather at an inspirational venue where there was something we could learn, as well as mix and mingle and get to know each other over cocktails and canapes. For example, we once started at the Big Data show at the Art Science Museum in Singapore, where the curator gave us a personal tour of the exhibit. Another time, a private tour at the Shanghai Modern Art Museum, where we had a play with some of the Augmented and Virtual Reality exhibits, was equally intriguing and inspiring.

The following day was split into four sessions, each focused on a different topic or digital challenge.

But models like this will likely need to be adapted for today's socially distanced and virtually enabled world. Below I share a suggested approach leveraging easily available tools and requiring no special expertise.

Introducing new members and getting to know each other

There are of course numerous ways this can be done; organisers upload a bio (*a bit boring*), participants write a short intro and share by email (*yawn*). Hold on! What about our theme of getting digital by digital? Let's at least do a Zoom call a week before and get everyone to introduce themselves. Let's do virtual ice breakers – how does "two truths and a lie" sound as a way to introduce yourself on Zoom? Don't know? Why not try it? Now is the time for experimentation.

A simple answer could be to challenge people to make and upload a short intro video and give recognition and kudos for the best efforts – someone will always surprise you and inspire others.

Sharing agenda and objectives (should be distributed and/or downloadable in advance).

The overall agenda can be split between strategic outlook and challenge statements.

In a day you can probably cover three or four topics, though personally I found going deeper into three to be more effective.

The **Strategic Outlook** session covers both internal and external experts providing insights and inspiration in terms of the latest technological and/or societal trends likely to affect the business. These can be futuristic, or of more immediate impact. Either way, it is ideal to have a combination of internal and external thought leaders, entrepreneurs disrupting the markets in which you operate, and even futurists giving a deeper look into what might come next. Obviously this can be delivered by Zoom, or even pre-recorded if necessary, though ideally you want these people to stay for the interaction in the next part.

This should then be followed by a breakout session, again by Zoom, where mixed teams of internal and external people discuss the potential threats offered but also technological breakthroughs, startup disrupters or societal changes. And then consider how to turn these threats into opportunities and disrupt yourselves before you are disrupted.

Teams should then reconvene on the main Zoom channel to share findings and recommendations. It is critical that someone from the core team is capturing this as you go along (with everyone's permission record all the meetings of course), and summarising as you go.

This is not intended as an academic exercise, but rather a catalyst to identify real initiatives that need to be launched and driven. This is where the internal team steps forward and takes responsibility to report back at the next DAB meeting, and also asks relevant advisers to contribute to the project moving forward, if relevant. This allocation of resources makes initial identification of topics critical to ensure that they align with growth priorities.

Having said that, it is also useful, once a year, to do a session that is completely blue sky thinking with no expectations of new products or enhanced productivity, just to stimulate some crazy ideas and see where they go. Invite your most 'edgy and controversial' external advisers or guest speakers for this one!

The real work however gets done in the **Challenge**

Statement sessions. Here, a senior business owner shares a customer, market or product challenge they are facing, and they or their team provides a full market/situation brief. A pre-selected external Advisor then shares an outside-in perspective, which may be from another industry, another market, or how, for example, blockchain is transforming that whole sector....Again, it can all be done by Zoom, but it is essential that all stay around for the breakouts.

The breakout teams then leverage design thinking approaches to consider various ways to address these challenges, propose new products, or how to enter new markets. The reason I prefer three rather than four sessions in a day, is that I like to spend more time and go deeper on each challenge, Ideally to get people building quick prototypes, that they can share to inspire the other teams.

In a fun session with the Asia-Pacific HR Leadership Team of Moet Hennessy a couple of years ago, we had everyone build a prototype in a morning. This transformed both their confidence in terms of Digital Mindset, but also created some really exciting new ideas for products and services customers might love!

A great tool for this, which anyone can use almost immediately, is the Marvel prototyping App. It's so simple even really senior people can use it. A couple of years ago we had the top 200 Managing Directors of DBS Bank in Singapore pair up and create 100 prototypes in a single morning.

Outcomes

Done right, a Digital Advisory Board, run as above, can generate an amazing amount of insight, innovation and inspiration in just a 24-hour period. You can address and make progress on some really thorny business challenges, and create some really compelling new ideas to be tested and validated.

This last point is critical. You don't end up with "answers".

You create ideas to test and validate. The core team and the business leader sponsoring each challenge, now need to follow through and develop an MVP and run a series of experiments to get validated learnings and enough data to decide which ideas are worth moving forward with. Reporting back to the next DAB meeting is important, though these days I'd recommend accelerating the cycle by having more frequent online check-ins, and ideally a monthly follow up.

If you think this sounds like too much work, then you likely didn't clearly identify real business challenges and priorities in the first instance. The DAB is a way to better anticipate trends, understand customer needs (Jobs To Be Done), and more quickly prototype and develop real products and services. A DAB is not a "nice to do" activity: it should be a way to improve the business and drive growth.

A very positive side effect of a good DAB, is that you also accelerate the "Digital Mindset" and confidence of those participating and other stakeholders. Making rotations of internal people through the DAB is a great people developer and should be part of your overall Digital Mindset strategy.

Sounds too big, too tough, too expensive? Start small...

One of the most critical success factors behind digital transformation and innovation in general, is a spirit of experimentation. Think you can't afford, organise or manage a Digital Advisory Board? Don't. Start much smaller, even on a personal level.

Do you have your own "Board of Advisers": friends, mentors and coaches that help you in your career? It can be simple to add a few people from the digital world. You can befriend some entrepreneurs. Offer to coach them on business, leadership or HR in return for them coaching you on Digital.

Start with a simple series of online fireside chats or webinars with leading entrepreneurs and disrupters in your field. Evolve overtime to a fuller DAB as described above. Just experiment, try stuff and see what works. Do it now. Send a calendar invite to the three most inspiring 'digital' people you know for a quick one on one next week, I'm sure at least one of them will do your first webinar with you.

Start today – experiment now – build your own virtual DBA – what's the DAB MVP look like? Where's your personal DAB?

8. Leaders – transform thyselves

Whether you are working from home or still in the office, working 50% or 150%, you also have an opportunity (*nay*, an obligation I would argue) to take some of this time to re-invent yourself as well.

I suddenly find myself at a loose end,. Having just finished a gig building the top team and launch organisation for a new Digital Bank in Dubai, I became effectively unemployed just as Corona struck. Thankfully, some dear friends and mentors on my own "Digital Advisory Board" have poked, prodded, provoked, and inspired me to use this time to re-invent myself.

So I'm in the process of converting my popular two-day Workshop on Digital Mindset and Innovation Culture that I used to deliver in person at conferences, to a fully virtual format that can be delivered to intact Leadership or HR teams over two to 10 days. I've never done this before – it's a new challenge and I'm learning lots of new things.

I've also been inspired by the incredible story of **Uma Rudd Chia** who wrote "10 Things Brands could do to Survive a Crisis" in 24 hours, I'm writing this book (in a little more than 24 hours!) in the hopes of being equally useful to leaders and HR teams around the world.

What are you doing to re-invent yourself?

The reality is that the Future of Work is here to stay, now. Digitisation is happening faster than ever. Expectations of leaders in terms of agility and adaptability, as well as empathy and engagement, have never been higher. When we all return to work, there will be a "new normal," whatever that means.

But without doubt, those that are more digitally literate, more able to think like a startup, more able to design and run experiments, and lead with empathy AND data, will be more likely to thrive and survive.

How do you rate yourself?

At my conference workshops (these days online!) I remind people that the CEO and leaders of their organisation are making decisions that influence not just the future growth of the company, but also their own careers, pensions, and their ability to put their kids through college…

Then, I ask people to close their eyes, and think about their leadership team. The CEO, COO, CTO, CIO, CHRO and other C-levels, and honestly ask, where would they rate them on a scale of one to 100 in terms of really "getting it" in terms of digital literacy?

Are they in denial? Doing symbolic stuff that really doesn't change things? Or are they really driving strategic digital transformation?

Next, I ask them to line up along the front of the conference room, standing in the place representing their assessment of their leadership team from one to 100. Then, I just let them look around, see who else is where, and think about the implications as they see some competitors ahead, some behind, and some different industry players in unexpected places.

It is always a sobering exercise.

Now you do it. Both for your CEO and leadership team, and

for yourself! Where do you rate your CEO on digital literacy and transformation? And honestly, where do you rate yourself?

If either of you are not in the top quartile, then you have fantastic data that it's definitely time to reinvent yourself – or to step forward and help transform your organisation.

If you want a better way to assess yourself and your organisation, you can find an article I wrote in late 2018 that will help: "**Readiness to digitise: 12 questions to ask first.**" This will help you quickly assess where you are on the journey and how well prepared your organisation is for what comes next.

So, what next?

It was probably **Clayton Christensen**, author of the famous **'Innovators Dilemma'** that first said that you will either *"disrupt yourself or be disrupted"* and it is the quote I find myself most often using as my conference speech tagline, or key workshop takeaway. The reality is that if you don't learn, change, adapt and innovate faster than the competition, a startup will disrupt your industry, and a robot, AI or more agile colleague will disrupt your job.

I am often asked at conferences how people can disrupt and transform themselves, how they can accelerate and strengthen their own digital mindsets, and ultimately, how can they increase their own competitiveness and market value?

Here are some ideas and easy ways to start on your own personal digital reinvention based on what I have found works really well for me. This is just intended to give you a nudge and inspiration to find what works for you.

Subscribe

Two awesome magazines, I've been reading both since their very first issues.

Wired magazine

Wired is a fun read that looks broadly at how technology is changing all aspects of society, art, politics, culture and business.

Fast Company magazine

Fast Company, dives deeper into how organisations are innovating, disrupting and evolving, and the impact of technology to accelerate this.

Read

The four most thought provoking books I've read recently.

Augmented: Life in the Smart Lane, by Brett King of Breaking Banks fame.

Exponential Organisations, Why new organisations are ten times better, faster and cheaper than yours (and what to do about it) by Salim Ismail

The Future is Faster than you think, how Converging Technologies are Transforming Business, Industries, and our Lives, by Peter Diamandis.

Founder of the xPrize and Singularity University – (I strongly recommend following him).

Gig Mindset: Reclaim your time, Reinvent your Career, and Ride the Next Wave of Disruption, by Paul Estes.

Completely re-set how I think about getting things done and escaping from the feeling of drowning in the quicksand of everyday corporate life – endless meetings and constant email. (I wish I'd read it before I started the book!)

Watch

My two favourite shows on cool advances in technology and innovations in Silicon Valley

BBC Click
Bloomberg Technology

Learn

I would recommend learning about Design Thinking, Lean StartUp, and Agile, to at least a conversational level of ability. There are many planning platforms/options out there.

Join – If you have the budget, look at **Abundance 360** or **Abundance Digital** (Peter Diamandis and Singularity University).

'Visit' – as many Innovation, entrepreneur & startup events as you can.

Partner – with disruptive startups in your industry, even if only from a learning perspective.

Contribute/Mentor

Find startups that interest you, align with your your passion or purpose, even if outside of work, and offer to mentor them, and/or make introductions of them. You will find there are a lot of two way sharing and learning opportunities.

Build

Create your personal Digital Advisory Board. One the last few years, I've found a few inspirational people that I like to catch up with whenever I can and learn from. Some of them are also kind enough to share their ideas and advice when I reach out on specific ideas or simple need someone to ask where to start on a new learning journey.

This is not a formal group, we do not meet, in fact some of the people have never met each other and don't even know that they are in my 'virtual' advisory board in my mind, but they are my go to people on all things digital, data and design!

Start

If you can't find it, start it. Years ago in Tokyo I wanted to learn more about CleanTech and Sustainability so I founded GreenMondays to gather monthly with experts I could learn from. It became a powerful community. Likewise in Singapore, some years ago I created a small group of thought leaders and practitioners in my field to meet occasionally and swap ideas. It's evolved through several iterations and is now know as 'Disruptive Drinks' and is strictly invitation only for people who are interesting, provocative, open to sharing, and doing something disruptive be it in corporate, startup, govt or NGO.

Be the person to start something and you will be known as 'Mr GreenMondays' in Tokyo. Or 'Mr Disruptive Drinks' in Singapore.

A good friend of mine, **Ben Whitter** has taken this to the extreme. Not only did he, literally, write the (bestselling) book on 'Employee Experience' and become known as 'Mr Employee Experience' but he even trademarked himself as 'Mr Employee ExperienceTM' and has subsequently launched and successfully grown the **World Employee Experience Institute**!

Employee Experience: Develop a Happy, Productive and Supported WorkForce for exceptional Individual and Business Performance

Don't wait for permission — build it, start it, make it yourself.

9. HR Leaders transform thyself (even more!)

Over the last 15 years, HR has been constantly criticised as underdelivering on both its promise and potential.

- In 2005, **Fast Company** magazine published its shocking – yet seminal – article entitled **"Why we Hate HR!"**

- In 2014, **Ram Charan** argued **"It's time to split HR"**

- In 2015, **Peter Capelli** in **HBR** explained **"Why We Love to Hate HR…and What HR Can Do About It."**

- In 2015, **Ram Charan** suggested we "Blow up HR" in **HBR**

- In 2015, **Dave Ulrich** responded to say **"Don't blow up HR, appreciate it and evolve it"**

- In 2016, **Forbes** added **"10 Reasons Everybody Hates HR"**

For more than two decades HR thought leader Professor Dave Ulrich has been encouraging HR to step forward and get a seat at the leadership table; for HR to be a more effective strategic business partner (Strategic Positioner); to think and operate "Outside-In"; and to be a partner to the CEO.

However, in many of my conference speeches and workshops in the last few years I have shown figures that show HR has still been under-delivering. For example, a large global survey of HR that I saw indicated that there was still a significant gap between the expectations of the CEO and the capabilities of HR.

The top priorities for CEOs were: developing an organisation for the digital world; driving digital transformation; and developing future ready digital leaders. Disturbingly, the biggest gap between leaders perception of HR and HR's perception of itself was the "ability to work in a highly digital environment" – with the majority of HR people self assessing as being uncomfortable, or not ready, to work in such an operating environment!

Indeed, I often shared that when I was reinventing myself as an HR person driving Digital Transformation, and working to create an innovation culture, I felt lonely – and often wondered if I was on the wrong track. At the time, I was attending as many startup, founder and entrepreneur, and innovation events as I could.

I felt compelled to understand these strange new technologies and ways of working. How did startups really work? How did entrepreneurs really think? How could they be so agile and innovative, and pivot so quickly? What was the secret of the mythical unicorns? (Startups with a US$1B valuation).

At these events I would find business people young and old looking to learn and be inspired to launch new products and businesses or acquire new partners. I saw technology people keen, in fact usually anxious, to reinvent themselves on cloud, data and AI. But what I never, ever saw, was another HR person. HR was missing in action from all these conferences and events.

I remember one particularly poignant moment when there was a major HR conference on in Singapore the exact same days that **InnovFest UnBound** was on. In Suntec City Conference Centre, you had 3,000 to 5,000 HR people talking about HR, while a mile away, you had over 10,000 innovators, entrepreneurs, scientists, business people, and founders, talking about exponential and transformational technologies that were fundamentally going to change society, life, business and work.

I could not help feeling that the HR people were in the wrong place.

I spent those days shuttling backward and forwards in Uber as I was speaking at the HR event, but spending all my time at InnovFest. The scariest thing was that none of the other HR people even knew what InnovFest was — Asia's largest Innovation event.

To give credit to the HR event organisers, **Domenica DeCrea**, **Emma Dean** & **Joanna Bush**, they took notice and innovated by launching the 'Smart WorkForce' event the following year.

Here are some of my reflections from the journey at the time, which I think will trigger some real introspection and reflections for any HR people reading this.

https://www.linkedin.com/pulse/digital-transformation-how-hr-can-get-personal-journey-smith/

HR Step Forward

In my speeches and workshops I always ended by exhorting HR leaders to step forward; to "get digital" themselves, to transform their teams and function; and to be the main partner to the CEO in transforming the culture of the organisation to be fit and agile and ready to compete in this brave new digital world.

Well, no more.

Ironically the burning platform of Covid 19 has helped HR jump the curve and close the gap. The Future of Work is here. Digital Transformation is now just how work gets done — and HR has indeed stepped forward.

HR, in partnership with IT, Marketing and Communications, and Facilities Managements and Finance, have all had to step forward and collaborate as never before in this crisis situation to keep us all safe and productive.

HR has had to simultaneously rethink remote working, co-ordinating and managing. To rethink how to engage employees spread all over the world who are simultaneously distracted by supporting elderly parents and home-schooling kids. There is a whole new world of **VEX** (Virtual Employee Experience) out there to be refined and defined, and a total rethink on how performance management and compensation works.

Facebook, Google, and more recently Salesforce and Twitter, have already declared that employees may choose to work form home until the end of the year. Presumably, many more companies will follow suit. Indeed, new data from IBM suggests that only a minority of people may return full-time to their workplaces. This creates a very different reality for HR to manage, and very different expectations of our leaders.

One probable consequence, highlighted by **Kevin Wheeler's** most recent **Future of Talent Institute** newsletter, is the flattening of organisations.

As of yesterday, many managers were engaged in managing people, often primarily as a coordination, risk and control activity: to make sure they were doing what they were supposed to be doing, when and where they were supposed to be doing it.

Much of that, traditionally "manual" coordination is now being managed virtually; there are greater levels of transparency and collaboration than even before, and the old managing by presence is a service or skill, in increasingly rapid decline.

Ref:
http://newsletters.futureoftalent.org/issues/future-of-talent-institute-weekly-issue-61-246175

As an example of an HR leader who is constantly re-inventing themselves – A close friend who's career journey in HR has been a constant journey of re-invention and transformation, has become known as **'the HR Chameleon'** due to his innate ability to identify and anticipate trends and their impact on the business.

Ommar Butt has held roles in most parts of HR, in multiple industries in both Europe and Asia and is currently Global head of People Analytics at Philips in Amsterdam. You can see my interview with him in HRMAsia magazine April 2018 at the link below.

http://media.licdn.com/embeds/media.html?src=https%3A%2F%2Fissuu.com%2Fhrmasia%2Fdocs%2Fhrm_apr_2018&url=https%3A%2F%2Fissuu.com%2Fhrmasia%2Fdocs%2Fhrm_apr_2018%2F58&type=text%2Fhtml&schema=issuu

https://www.linkedin.com/in/ommar/

HR – a step further – platforms & ecosystems

Paradoxically, the timing has never been better for HR.

HR now not only has a seat at the table and higher-than-ever credibility with the CEO, but also the moral authority and situational opportunity to transform our organisations faster than ever before.

This is truly HR's time to make a difference and help accelerate positive systemic changes in our organisations, institutions, and our very society.

Different people have suggested this crisis may actually be "The Great Reset" or a "Great Transformation" and have talked about a shift away from an obsessive focus on shareholder returns towards broader stakeholder management.

I think this is inevitable as companies are no longer taking up big office blocks downtown or in isolated business parks, but even the world's largest and most powerful companies are now dispersed in every village, town, suburb and city. We now all live and work in the very communities we serve. Will we still be able to ignore the externalities of waste, pollution and climate change as so many companies long have? Will the imbalance in diversity and representation on Corporate Boards be allowed to continue? Will the increasingly large wealth gaps between the haves and have nots be able to continue to broaden so obnoxiously?

Increasingly the role of HR will be to bring people together to work in virtual global teams where we blend employees, gig economy freelancers, and other partners into teams and projects of various duration. Our suitability for projects will be judged not so much by our positional power or seniority, but by our reputation, ratings, and reviews within and between organisations and in a broader global marketplace of talent.

For every new task, project, business, or departmental or geographical expansion, consider creating options for the business leaders in terms of staffing and resourcing. Offer a mix of full-time staff and part time staff, as well as contractors and gig economy free agents. Experiment and explore: how virtual can you go? You obviously need to be mindful of intellectual property, confidentiality and compliance, but I bet you can surprise yourself in how creative you can get.

On simple project is to do A/B testing to see how far you can go. Amazon, Google, Facebook et al use A/B testing continuously to assess which option is best based on real customer interactions and data. At the simplest, this can be changing the colour or position of a button on a website. Or it could be presenting different options to similar audiences and seeing which one they really want to buy before you commit to inventing and building.

Think about to what extent you can do A/B testing in HR projects. Can you run small experiments to get data from your (internal) customers before proposing a solution? Can you build a quick prototype or MVP with them to decide which solution works best? How can you apply startup thinking to HR?

With some of these experiments they will allow you to test some of your craziest ideas without risk. Even if they are in mission critical areas, you can typically build simple prototypes and experiments to run alongside the existing processes until you get enough data to justify an investment and switchover.

Offering options based on data

Imagine if HR offers leaders a spectrum of resourcing models, leveraging the best of internal and external talent based on their reputation, ratings and reviews? See the next chapter for how this can develop, but for now start to think how HR could offer a variety of resourcing models leveraging the best talent from anywhere. While the obvious advantages may be reduced headcount and fixed costs – the advantages of greater real-time access to more responsive and innovative expertise may be the real benefit.

HR should also do all of the above to develop themselves, but also find their own HR thought leaders to follow, those at the leading edge of how the future of work and technology is impacting your business and customers. Engage with them and bring them into your ecosystem, offer to share your experiments with them or give them access to your most exciting projects on leadership and culture in return for their thought leadership.

Two I like to follow are:

Josh Bersin of http://joshbersin.com
and
Jeanne Meister of Future Workplace

As more and more of our work output and work processes become largely, or fully, digitised, and as the friction of co-ordination costs, management by presence, and bureaucracy are reduced, work will increasingly become near real-time and we will have more data than ever before.

10. Explore Data, Platforms, and Ecosystems

Transparency

There will be a greater than ever level of transparency into work effort, productivity, collaboration, effectiveness and impact. Ironically, with a move away from *"management by presence"* we will move towards *"management by participation"*. As more and more of our work takes place online and is digitised or recorded, it will be both more visible and more measurable.

This increase in transparency of effort and impact and will be hugely encouraging to unsung heroes and the quiet introverts that used to put in extra effort and never got recognised for it. Likewise, for those who excel at managing up, but perhaps don't deliver quite as much as their quieter peers, life could suddenly be a lot less comfortable.

Over time, this increased transparency will have a profound impact on corporate culture; and strengthen the need for Purpose-driven organisations, strong and aligned values and behaviours, and leaders who lead by example, as discussed in earlier chapters.

Another interesting consideration when we think about

"management by participation" in terms of being judged by those you work for, the new reality is that the better talent will have more choices.

People will increasingly be able to choose where they work, who they work with, and, most importantly for organisations, which company they work for. We will look into this more later when we talk about platforms and ecosystems but bear in mind that greater transparency goes both ways, and both employees and gig economy partners may increasingly choose to work for and deliver their talent where it is the most appreciated, and to organisations that match their values and enable them to live their life's purpose.

Measurement

Increasingly virtual and digital organisations will be more transparent, leading to greater personal accountability that will also, from a business impact perspective, be more measurable. The good news is that while the old reality of "what gets measured gets managed" begins to apply to everything, we also face being overwhelmed with data and a level of information access that we may not be prepared for. At the very least, this will demand a much greater level of **data literacy** from all of us, but especially from our leaders.

This probably demands another chapter to explore, but let me leave you a live example that I was recently involved with. I've spent the last 15 months as the Chief HR Officer at a new Digital Bank soon to launch in Dubai. Uniquely among fully digital challenger banks, they are launching both retail and corporate banking simultaneously and have digitised the entire organization. We consciously designed for "zero people", though in reality we expected to have about a quarter of the people of a traditional bank for an equivalent volume of revenue.

Our blueprint for the launch team of what I called the

'**Minimal Viable Bank**' was set at 100 people, as we curated an ecosystem of partners, rather than building a complex and expensive core banking system.

But what is most relevant here is that we digitally encoded the entire DNA of the bank from the very beginning. While this is difficult and expensive for existing organisations to do, if you are doing a spinout or startup, seriously consider it. We used an Enterprise Architecture Software to capture and encode every single process, policy, product, principle and person in the bank.

We mapped the data flow of the entire customer journey. And every single element was mapped to every element it touched. This both gave us a real-time window into the bank's operations, as well as the ability to model a change and see exactly how that would flow through the business, from marketing, to customer touch points, to technology, to operations.

This real-time view of the bank, was one we could even share with auditors or the central bank. It also made us realise that we needed to start to think very differently about how we motivated, engaged, measured, and rewarded people.

The dilemma I faced at the time was how to create and nurture a startup culture of risk taking and experimentation in a highly regulated banking entity.

In some ways this was just a pre-cursor to the questions most leaders will have to struggle with in 2020 and beyond: how do we manage, engage and measure the performance of our workforce when a majority may be working virtually?

One of the key ways is to reframe our traditional notions of the employee value proposition, these days, more typically described as the Employee Experience (or EX) with newly-developing notions of **VEX**, the Virtual Employee Experience. Increasingly whether people are employees, partners or free agent giggers, they are still looking for purpose and meaning in their work, as well as an income.

Moving forward, the most successful organisations will be those that can attract and engage the best talent from both inside and outside the organisation. This will lead to a now notion of the traditional "Give-Get" model of the employee contract to a broader and more inclusive model of *"Contribution and Actualisation."*

Note that a key difference here is the move away from the largely extrinsic motivation model of you *give* me your time and effort, and you will *get* paid for it, to a mode of more intrinsic motivation. This is a situation where you both contribute to something you care about, and get a sense of self-actualisation from it, as well as getting paid, either in salary or fees.

This very much aligns with **Dan Pink's** work on **Drive: The Surprising Truth About What Motivates Us**, mentioned above. That shares the reality long known by psychologists but ignored as inconvenient or difficult to work with by managers and HR: that beyond a certain level of hygiene factor income, people are more motivated by intrinsic motivation than purely monetary rewards.

Value and reputation marketplaces

As organisations become increasingly virtual and digitalised, Talent is going to seek its own 'best value' and most natural fit. As Daniel Pink reminds us, people are motivated by "mastery", "autonomy", and "purpose". Now I am not suggesting that everyone will quit big companies and full-time jobs and all become freelancers overnight, but there is a clear trend in that direction over time that this crisis has only accelerated.

Ultimately, both within and between organisations, people will be increasingly valued by their **3Rs**.

With virtual organisations, digitally enabled work, and data-driven transparency, people will be valued and rated by their **Reputation, Ratings and Reviews**. Some of these will be internal, some external, and some private to certain platforms, memberships or associations.

Much like today, organisations have a reputation in the marketplace, a Gallup or other Employee Engagement ranking, and Glassdoor or similar employee (user) driven ratings, so it will become with individual employees. For example, to get the cover of this book designed, I engaged three different designers on fiverr.com based on their reputation, previous ratings and reviews and overall ranking on the website, had them each submit their best ideas, and finally choose the cover you see.

So if talent, be they employees or freelancers, are increasingly valued by their visible and measurable output and impact, how do you attract the best and where will they choose to work?

To quote "Joy's Law", first mentioned by Bill Joy, Founder of Sun MicroSystems, when referring to their Java Strategy in 1995, *"the smartest people in the world don't all work for us. Most of them work for someone else."*

What we are seeing today is the emergence, accelerated by this crisis, of a global, virtual marketplace for talent that will be driven by the 3Rs. Indeed a recent article by the BBC argued that **"education is the new currency"** and there are various blockchain based startups trying to create platforms to enable this.

Ref:
https://www.bbc.com/worklife/article/20200210-is-education-the-new-currency

What are the implications for leaders and HR?

While you can always pay for talent, it seems clear that we are gradually moving towards a "talent-based economy" where people are not only earning enough to live, but also striving to achieve their life purpose.

If that sounds like a paradox, it is more a new way of looking at organisations.

I think we will see a spectrum of organisational forms, from the traditional forms we are used to, to new organisational forms that are still evolving and emerging.

At one end of the spectrum we will have traditional, slow-moving command and control organisations that are low trust and low innovation, but high control, and I think these will disappear over time. While at the other extreme, a gig economy or free-agent world where people pursue their passions and sell their capabilities to the highest bidder.

Somewhere in the middle of that spectrum, I think we will see the emergence of new organisational forms. These are high in trust, purpose and innovation, and will require a very different leadership mindset and skillset to lead — it is a form that I believe will thrive post-crisis and become dominant over the next 20 to 30 years.

These are "Exponential Organisations★" that are growing and scaling exponentially compared with traditional organisations. They are driven by Massive Transformative Purposes (MTP) that attract the best talent, both full-time employees and the best external agents and giggers from the global ecosystem. They aggressively leverage emerging exponential technologies, and have a growth mindset of continuous experimentation.

These organisations may have a core of dedicated full-time employees, but they will be complemented by a constellation of aligned external partners and free agent or gigger resources operating "on demand" and attracted by the organisation's purpose as well as the opportunity to learn and contribute.

Ref:
★https://www.amazon.com/Exponential-Organizations-or-ganizations-better-cheaper-ebook/dp/B00OO8ZGC6/ref=sr_1_1?crid=F4EEM9I18409&dchild=1&keywords=ex-

ponential+organizations&qid=1589952731&s=digital-text&spre-
fix=expone%2Caps%2C403&sr=1-1

How do you prepare?

Firstly, if you haven't worked out your own Purpose yet,
either read Nick Craig's latest book and do the exercises,
or watch Peter Diamandis on MTP and define your own
Life Purpose or MTP.

The simplest way is to try tiny experiments and learn as
you go. Design for yourself a learning journey that lets you
experiment with ecosystems and platform thinking, with gig
economy services, and with ways to achieve your purpose,
both at work and beyond.

Next time you need a project doing, put a (non-sensitive)
version of it out to bid, even if it's just your powerpoint
slides, or creating a poster or brochure to start with. Later,
as you learn, try something more complex like designing a
new product or identifying a new molecule, the reality is
that in open innovation competitions, external teams from
the community and crowd, nearly always beat a team of
internal experts.

If you think that your company is too regulated to do this,
know that GE & NASA among many others sue this approach.

Again, do this as A/B testing so you minimise your risk.
Give the same objectives to your own internal team, then
post the challenge on some open innovation or gig economy platform. And see which team comes up with the best
solution. This is a low cost, low risk way to try out some
talent in your organisations nebulous emergent ecosystem
and see if anyone is attracted to what you're doing.

This type of testing gives you a quick reality check on the
strengths of your internal people and what their development
needs might be, but also allows you to attract and engage
with the best talent out there in any particular field. The good
news is you no longer need to rush out there and hire them

to lock them in, but you better have a compelling sense of organsational purpose to attract and retain them, as well as a well-developed way to attract and engage external talent.

The reality is that you can no longer think of your "organisation" as what's on the org chart. This has been not only wrong for years, but also useless, as informal networks within the organisation have done their own things. These days, it is positively dangerous.

Try a new model. Try thinking of your organisation as an ecosystem of projects, ideas, resources and capabilities who coalesce and align to achieve certain projects and deliverables. Some will be core resources who attract others to their projects, and others will be flexible resources, both internal and external, that join projects that appeal to them. There will be a natural balance achieved over time as people seek to balance their need for income with their desire to make a contribution.

I think the reality is that this crisis has pulled people together even as it has enforced social distancing and demanded remote working. I think it may have left us more human, more open, and more tolerant.

The most critical new leadership skill will be managing these ecosystems of employees, partnerships and giggers, in a way that is both inspiring and engaging, supported and enabled by increasingly sophisticated tools, bots and AI agents.

It will be necessary to envisage and bring to life a whole new way of operating, a **'Virtual Ecosystem Experience'** to complement our 'Virtual Employee Experience.'

'Quite possibly it will be the successful blend of virtual employee experience with virtual ecosystem experience that will differentiate tomorrow's winners from the losers.'

Warning. Dead-end ahead

Above I've talked a lot about experimentation, prototyping

and working with startups. In some ways, this is really easy – just try it and learn as you go. Although if you can find mentors for the journey as discussed above, you will enhance your chances for success.

However at the same time, most organisations have strong compliance, risk and control functions specifically designed to prevent people from "breaking things" that could impact the business either financially or reputation wise. And for very good reason.

Be warned that if you are partnering with, or learning from startups – as a big corporate, you can literally talk them to death and/or strangle them with red tape. Aim for minimal viable experiments with the minimum of risk to both sides, and iterate quickly as you get data and proof of concept.

Startups have a limited runway based on their cash reserves, and operate at a very different speed to big corporates. A bit like butterflies, they may be beautiful, but can have a very short life span if they engage with big corporates that waste their time with copious amounts of IT requirements, and unreasonable compliance demands.

You need to apply common sense as to where experimentation is and is not appropriate, as well as where to proactively engage with the Compliance, Risk, IT, Procurement and HR functions to get them onboard.

In one amazing example, **Jimmy Ng**, then Head of Internal Audit for DBS Bank, decided to "Make Audit Joyful" in line with the Bank's new purpose back in 2016. Needless to say, he earned a lot of scepticism at the time. However, after a whole series of imaginative and innovative initiatives, he truly transformed how Audit was perceived, making it a more proactive function that engaged early as a thought-partner in what was possible – and allowable, as the rest of the bank engaged with startups and conducted over 100 experiments in a year! This goes to show that even the most traditionally conservative of business functions can innovate and can advance with the digital age.

A couple of years later, Jimmy took over as Chief Technology Officer, and Head of Technology and Operations with responsibility for a third of the Bank's workforce.

Final thoughts

A final thought first on open ecosystems: – as we increasingly work and collaborate globally, while travelling less, we are actually breaking down barriers faster than ever. To compete effectively we cannot win with closed systems, or closed mindset "me-first" thinking.

Instead, we have the opportunity to create truly inclusive global organisations, no matter their size, that are open to talent from anywhere and welcoming to all members and anyone who can contribute. This could be the greatest opportunity ever to accelerate and celebrate all forms of diversity, as alignment with Purpose and Values, and contribution and impact matter more than anything else.

My opinion was just re-inforced by a blog post I saw today from one of my favourite commentators on all things financial and FinTech, **Chris Skinner**, commenting on Jamie Dimon's comment that the "Corona Virus must lead to a more inclusive society"

Ref:

https://thefinanser.com/2020/05/coronavirus-must-lead-to-a-more-inclusive-society-says-jamie-dimon.html/

A final thought also for readers who are **HR leaders**. Now is the time for HR to step forward, to create human places to work, belong, contribute to, and grow. You need to look up and out, not just down and in to your traditional HR tasks.

HR needs to "get digital" in terms of startup thinking and "Digital Mindset" quicker than any other part of the organisation to properly play its role. To quote a good friend,

Pushdeep Gupta of Deloitte's Global Leadership Practice, we need to *"startup-ify HR"*.

Throughout this crisis HR has worked closer than ever with the CEO and the rest of the management team. The positive trends and changes resulting from this pandemic have the possibility to be a massive accelerator for the ability of business and organisations to make a difference and contribute to society beyond a simple profits first and only mentality.

HR can now be a critical enabler to help make more human organisations and ecosystems that can leverage technology to enhance people and create more meaningful and high impact workplaces and experiences. HR has never had a better chance to have an impact. So step forward and act now, for the sake of the organisation, for your families and communities, and for the planet itself.

In the future, the most effective form of leadership will be all about creating and curating purpose driven ecosystems. Ideally you want to be the platform on which multiple ecosystems thrive.

To quote Google's revised rules of Innovation: "be a platform and float all boats"

10 Things in Summary

As a quick, easy to remember summary, here are the the 10 key ideas and takeaways:

1. **Start with Purpose** – and move away from managing by presence. When you have a clearly articulated organisational purpose you will attract talent that believes in it and their intrinsic motivation will drive them to contribute and perform. They won't need layers of managers, but will be inspired by purpose driven leaders.

2. **Update your Values for today's world**. Make sure that you actually have clearly defined and inspiring

values that drive real behaviour and are lived by your leaders and supported by your systems and, especially, HR processes.

3. **Transparency breeds Trust.** Your employees understand this is a crisis and are looking to your for leadership, but involve them in generating options and ideas and make them part of the solution.

4. **Try new models of employment & engagement.** Use this opportunity to free some of your employees to become free agents aligned with you, share them with partners and get closer to customers.

5. **Learn, Share & Experiment.** Engage under-utilised employees in learning, sharing and experimenting on new ways to solve customer's problems, innovate products and accelerate your organisations path to digital literacy and agility.

6. **Transform faster – 'Get Digital' now!** Quickly, design, launch and iterate on initiatives to increase Digital literacy across the organisation. This will generate confidence, experimentation and momentum and encourage and enable transformation more organically.

7. **Digital Advisory Boards go Digital.** Create even a simple form of virtual Digital Advisory Board, either for yourself as a leader, your team/function, or the whole organisation. Use them as advisers but also problem solvers and partners in innovation.

8. **Leaders – Transform thyselves.** As leaders we need to lead by example. We should each have a higher level of general digital literacy, awareness and aptitude to try new things than we can expect of our employees. Try some new, fun digital stuff, just explore and have fun.

9. **HR Leaders – Transform thyselves (more).** CEO's are expecting more than ever from HR, step forward,

take the initiative, implement 1 − 10 listed here! HR doesn't just have a seat at the table, HR is helping set the agenda for the future of the organisation.

10. **Explore Data, Platforms & Ecosystems.** Increasingly talent will be attracted and managed by Reputation, Ratings and Reviews. And so will you and the entire organisation which will require a greater focus on managing both Virtual Employee Experience and Virtual Ecosystem Experience of all your stakeholders.

Postscript

The idea of 'Virtual Eco-system Experience' (or VEX), of how to create and nurture ecosystems, emerged quite un-expect-edly as this book took form. I believe this could be a key leadership capa-bility of the future.

I think it requires deeper thinking and another ar-ticle or book to explore further. If you agree, please add a review or send a comment and let's make it happen.

About the Author

Laurence Smith, Chartered Fellow CIPD

Thought Leader in Digital Mindset & Transformation

L aurence is most recently the **Chief People Officer** (CHRO) of the world's first pure play universal digital bank, soon to launch in Dubai, UAE.

In this role, Laurence worked with the CEO, CTO & Chief Data Officer to completely re-think how a data-first digital bank operates, and the implications for organisation design, staffing & capabilities. The challenge was to create an innovative TechFin culture that is 100% compliant to today's Central Bank regulations, while also innovating into the future.

This required developing a Culture, Employee Value Proposition (EVP) and Employee Experience to attract the best digital, banking and technology talent from around the world and meld them into a cohesive organisation while meeting tough deadlines and managing investor expectations.

Prior to this, Laurence worked on and advised various **Digital Transformation** projects across Asia, and also contributed to the design and setup of national Digital *'Future Skills'* initiatives in Singapore and Thailand. He was also on the Digital Advisory Board of Danone Asia.

Previously Laurence was **Managing Director Human Resources and Group Head of Learning & Talent Development** at **DBS Bank** in Singapore. He is most recognised for his work with the CEO on defining the Bank's Purpose to '*Making Banking Joyful*' and the innovative & award winning *#DBSHackathon* series. The overall Digital Mindset initiative & associated hackathon series was credited with helping develop the innovation culture that led to DBS being recognised as the '*World's Best Digital Bank*' in 2016 and 2018. Laurence personally received the CEO's **Asian Banking Innovation Award** for this work.

Laurence is a frequent conference speaker, trainer, <u>writer and thought leader on Digital Mindset & Innovation Culture</u>, as well as a frequent mentor & judge at Hackathons, including the <u>Singapore Government's nationwide 'Skills Future' Hackathon</u>.

In recognition of his thought leadership and contribution to the field of HR, Laurence was in 2019 recognised as a **Fellow** of the **Chartered Institute of Personnel Development**.

A British national, Laurence has previously held senior roles as global Chief Learning Officer at LG Electronics in Seoul, APAC Head of Learning & Development for GE Money in Tokyo, & with the Organisation Design Practice at McKinsey in Boston. He has spent over 20 years in Asia and holds an MSc in Organisation Design & Knowledge Management from the US.

Laurence Smith LinkedIn Profile:
https://www.linkedin.com/in/laurencesmith/

Made in the USA
Columbia, SC
25 March 2022